The Mineral Point Poetry Series

Tanka & Me	Kaethe Schwehn
My Seaborgium	Alicia Rebecca Myers
Fair Day in an Ancient Town	Greg Allendorf
My Tall Handsome	Emily Corwin
A Wife Is a Hope Chest	Christine Brandel
Black Genealogy	Kiki Petrosino
The Rise of Genderqueer	Wren Hanks
This Is Still Life	Tracy Mishkin
Life on Dodge	Rita Feinstein
Calf Canyon	Sarah McCartt-Jackson

The Mineral Point Poetry Series 10 · Kiki Petrosino, Editor

CALF CANYON

poems

Sarah McCartt-Jackson

Brain Mill Press
Green Bay, Wisconsin

Some of the poems in this collection have appeared previously in the following publications and are reprinted here with permission:
> *The Maine Review*: "Nights" and "Animals"
> *Monolith*: "Interlude"
> *NANO Fiction*: "Creston"
> *Tidal Basin Review*: "Calf Canyon"

Copyright © 2018 by Sarah McCartt-Jackson.
All rights reserved.

Published in the United States by Brain Mill Press.
Print ISBN 978-1-948559-21-8
EPUB ISBN 978-1-948559-24-9
MOBI ISBN 978-1-948559-22-5
PDF ISBN 978-1-948559-23-2

Cover photograph "Manhattan, Forest Park, Queens New York, 2013" © Yoav Friedlander.
Cover design by Oona Miller.

www.brainmillpress.com

The Mineral Point Poetry Series, number 10.
Published by Brain Mill Press, the Mineral Point Poetry Series is edited by Kiki Petrosino. In odd years, the series invites submissions of poetry chapbooks around a theme. In even years, the editor chooses a full collection.

To Jason and Falinia, for renting the car.
To Bryan, who drove to Amarillo.

Contents

Foreword by series editor Kiki Petrosino   xiii

Calf Canyon
    Crossing   1
    Estuary   5
    Halocline   9
    Sound   13
    Crossing (*ii*)   16
    Estuary (*ii*)   20
    Halocline (*ii*)   24
    Sound (*ii*)   28

Homeplace   2
Westward Migration   3
Driving to the Vineyard   7
Drought   11
Wildfire   12
Creston   14
Merlot   15
Boy   18

What I Leave in Your Palms:	19
Chardonnay	21
Nights	22
Animals	25
Aubade	27
Pinot Noir	29
Crush	30
Author's Acknowledgments	33
About the Author	35

"I am trying to tell my unborn daughter a story," the speaker of Sarah McCartt-Jackson's *Calf Canyon* explains. Many pieces in this stunning collection begin with some version of this sentence. *Calf Canyon* is a compendium of unsent letters to this listening absence, a catalog of the silences that stitch up the speaker's world. Every story has a beginning, of course, but in McCartt-Jackson's poetry, one story can have several beginnings, each with its own mysterious beauty.

These poems deploy a variety of rich forms, from long-limbed free verse to highly textured prose blocks. The reader follows McCartt-Jackson's speaker down long, winding paths of memory, encompassing not only the origin story of the "unborn daughter" but the speaker's own emotional genesis. The waterside landscapes of rural Kentucky and the Ozarks give way to the dry gulches and deep ravines of California as the speaker attains adulthood and her relationships become more fraught with dangers of various types.

"Your father and I did love each other," the speaker assures her unborn beloved, "like black oystercatchers and their limpets." Who's the predator, and who the prey, in this retelling? Like all the best origin myths, each protagonist has a foil, their shared dynamic intense and irresistible as fate. In *Calf Canyon*, we need darkness and light, leaves and "leafshadows scrambling on their stems like starlings stuck to wire." The reality of the speaker's world only becomes concrete, palpable, when everything intangible—the air between dishes, the shade of an oak, even the mouth's reflection in the skin of a berry—is accounted for, and sung.

McCartt-Jackson's gifts as a music-maker transform these poems into eerie sonic landscapes. The reader momentarily lulled by the fairytale-like qualities of lines like "How a bullet. How a blade. / How silver will wink or shine or not" finds herself at the brink of peril in the poem "Nights." We shiver along with the speaker, recalling some violent encounter or slender escape. In these poems, memories are permeable landscapes, inviting the reader to enter.

The poems of *Calf Canyon* transport us to deeply personal spaces, but they also remind us of shared mysteries. We're called to witness the beginning of life and its too-quick terminus; the rush of passion and its aftermath; the silences that deepen like canyons over the wounds we carry. These are complex and necessary meditations, and McCartt-Jackson brings them, beautifully, to life.

Kiki Petrosino
Editor, Mineral Point Poetry Series

Calf Canyon

/ Crossing /

I am trying to tell my unborn daughter a story. It is an old story
that hangs on the spinneret tip of a spider's abdomen,

the spider's heart a bruise,
each chamber a stitch that nicks the copper blood
as it rushes through, each valve sighing out
                                              like the hush that hung

lodged in everyone's lungs,
       a silence stacked between plates on the drying rack,
a thrum that vibrated the blades of his kitchen knives.
       I had to hide under the trailer steps
the jaw of the shotgun I unloaded
       when I heard his truck tires coming,
       the unspent slugs plunked in the toilet tank.

My unborn child's story begins as the terrible budding star of a black widow,
her red eyes a speck glinting in the swamp cooler:

—.—

Homeplace
(Kentucky)

Here, an icicle melts into a pond of blue light,
                              opening mud, cake of earth shines

fishscale oilsheen, wrinkled rivershore

Nicks her fingernail on the broomhandle hickory
                coaldust in the quilt seams, in the floor scars

    Here, April sun distant-pale, April sun tart as an early apple

Here in the dusk cusp, deer know the storm-licked rims of drought

He the crunch between gravel and tire, she the peach

    pulp sucked from the woody pit ridges

Here, the chilly spring raw as a bruise
                            struck by the earth beneath its perfect limb.

Westward Migration
(California)

There was all the cold vodka and fresh-killed meat anyone could eat. There was a clothesline, like I had always wanted, a large back deck that overlooked nothing but acres of land. Acres of land I could walk before day burned its sand into glass. There was an oversized tub I filled with cold water on those 100-degree days, ice you could stab right off the freezer walls, a washer and a sink, running water, two shade-oak trees, windows on every wall, my own bathroom for when I wanted it. There was money enough for cigarettes, to drive the hour to the beach (too cold to get in), to pay for satellite to watch *Wheel of Fortune* from our deck, with the windows open, eating hot dogs, macaroni salad. There were people friendly enough to invite us for dinners, barbecues, make us lunches and offer free after-work beers from their truckbeds. There was land so open you could touch the dusty heart of a full blue moon at the top of a sand ridge. There were views, from the mission church with its terra-cotta accents, from the reservoirs into the well-irrigated orchards of peaches, avocados, plums, lemons, apples, grapes, grapes, grapes. There were birds in the shade trees, wind gusts that pushed us inside in laughter and breaks, while the Mexicans in the fields tied their hoodies tighter over their eyes. There were reservoirs to swim in, naked and blue, warm and cool on our skin. There were late nights lit by full moons where we would all gather like lonely quail, climb into a truck, and shoot something moving or drive into a ditch, ruin our bodies, just to make the air around us move, shudder, break. There was a post office inside the Long

4

Branch Bar. There was a library, or a room called a library. There were long, winding, one-lane roads that were fun to drive, but still had blood on them from wrecked bodies, split lives emptied of parties, people, food, music, guns, boots, falcons, trucks, plentiful water shipped in from a thousand miles, an ocean just over that ridge. No, just over that one. No, that one there.

| Estuary |

How do I tell my unborn daughter that once
the riverbed sang in ice thaw and rainswell,
sang with the groan and splash of a glacier chunk
pushing through the North Pacific Drift
        goaded by the tidal bulge dragging from the poles,
the edges of low tide delicate as paper wasp wings,
        the sea depths pulled up and swollen like a lens
as if this world itself were a visual organ, pulsing or squinting

sang with the groan contracting through the oval egg tidewaters,
        a pool forming somewhere in arctic black sand,
        an anemone sprouting in its wrackline,
fleshy-pink tentacles waving the sound along
        toward tributaries dilating like a beating artery

until the grumble settled as a stone of rain, dropped into the river,
        sank into the mud of this Camatta creekbed

until the tongue of summer licked it clean as sun
on cow skulls and bleached gypsum.

With each swallow, more continent silts its throat.

6

How to show her unformed eyes: a river choking itself
       with each sediment it lay down
in its bed, cracked and split like unslaked lips:

—.—

Driving to the Vineyard

starts with coffee, cold in Styrofoam cups
reheated from yesterday's pot. Always
a cigarette, even when I didn't want one.

His gray Ford Ranger that had crossed the Valley,
crossed the Rockies, crossed the Ozarks,
crossed the bridge straight out of Kentucky,
rumbled over the cattle strips, swerved
to hit squirrels or tarantulas in migration.

Too-loud music, too-cold breeze coming
in through the cracked windows, too-close
creekbed, dried up, filled with too many cattle
bones, coyote teeth, fossils that will never be
found. Too-bright sun, not enough visor.

But when we would crest the high ridge,
the sun rose into our windshield
like a different day, like a sand mandala
spilled just so, this pink on the fenceline,
this dawn-blue fog turning back
into grape leaves, this sudden burst

8

of vineyard greening the straw-dry chaparral,
so that for one minute I believed
there might be soil rich
as Kentucky forest loam, as if each hill,
sand-filled and thirsty, drank.

/ Halocline /

I am trying to tell my unborn daughter an old story. So I try:

My dearest,

Somewhere, not too far from here,
between the oat grass and junegrass of the shore,
between the giant wild rye and mudflats
suckling the uprooted algae beds of the estuaries,

your father and I did love each other
like black oystercatchers and their limpets.

Somewhere, our love was salt spray on the inlet rocks
where we both first heard you unmade yet,
your voice riming the mouths of the coastal caves at Montaña de Oro,
    your voice the kiss in our bellies
    as we snatched onto each other like thieves,
    as we swam with the riptide
        into the caves and water-lapped walls, his eyes
                      an echo
      to his rough hands, his love a pane
      of glass reflecting my face
      until he drew me in and bolted the lid shut.

Do you understand how eucalyptus skin peels
> so thin you want to snap it off and place it on your tongue?
> How the sweet green spoor tastes like coastal fog?

> How the strands of that forest saturate the home of live oak
> until the trees recede into saplings that struggle inside a rotting crevice
> the size of an embryo?

Do you understand spike-moss appears dead in dry seasons but will blush after rains?

> The tide was washing in. Your voice was the tide lub-dubbing in my ventricle.

And if you are in the caves when the sungold-tipped waves return,
> like a bride returning to her veil, you will drown:

—.—

Drought

It begins with drink. Our eyes drink color and reflect it back to our brains, which drink shape. Shape drinks shade, leafshadows scrambling on their stems like starlings stuck to wire. Wire drinks voices, spliced threads chopped apart and ribosomed back together in a winding ladder propped against our earlobes. Our earbones drink the wet sounds of leaves unfolding newborn fists, the desperate sound of fish gills in a boat bucket. Our hands drink the wormblood and hook. Our foreheads drink sweat, our forearms hair and knuckle. Our ankles the mosquito tongue, dry of our neighbor's blood. Boatplanks drink scales and shoe soles and cigarette ash and oceanfog and the heat of sunlogged turtles, which drink the cloverstem milk, which drinks the roothairs, which drink the cavelight, which drinks the batwing, drinks the limestone, drinks the fossilbone slipped between a molten stone harvest. The inner core drinks iron-tasting pennies, nickel. Not enough liquid in the world to fill its iron core. And this is how in drought I learn a rogue billet does not raise a doe's eye, how a doe does not lift from drinking.

Wildfire

We watched the fires spread.

Neighbors set up their lawn chairs

to watch their neighbors' houses burn.

Which is how I caught a bottle

to the face when I threw a cigarette

butt out the window. And how

the bottle shattered and fractured

the windshield after my jaw and how later

he didn't remember (or said he didn't)

how the windshield cracked,

and I told him,

and he said that wasn't true.

And so it wasn't true.

/ Sound /

My unborn girl could not be born

in those brittle hills that bulged like pregnant women
lying on their backs on crumpled bedsheet dunes
that swallowed me, pressed into a dark gulch
as mustard stem branched through my bones, stacking
its yellow skeleton chloroplast
by chloroplast into the gaps of my marrow:
                                    the land a groom
that saddled my pelvis, rooting the wings of my hips
into that dirt until I could nurse nothing
but dust and fossils plucked from the extinct
shorebeds of Camatta Creek:
                    a thirsty slit between the canyon walls

powdered with the flaking ribs of cattle, shells broken
from their hinges, and a sand that sucked the mussels naked,
the tissue leeched into tarweed and hoary nettle.

I hear her voice: a resin gurgling just beneath the surface bark
of my skin, her voice: tiny fingernails scratching at the woody chaparral:

—.—

Creston

I did not see the moonwashed lake behind our trailer or the yellow finch in the avocado tree. I did not see the fire, the smoke of which we watched from the mustard thistle lawn. I did not see the coyotes eating the dead cattle or the California mouse while it was still alive. I did not see old Ted (all thirty-three and married) wreck on Shell Creek Road with a nineteen-year-old passenger in lip gloss and cutoffs, when it was not just ten days before he took me to a baby's grave on our way back from buying a pack of cigarettes, and me seventeen. The freeze on the vineyard edges. The lizard drinking from the wild pig bleed. The shotgun slug through the throat of a barn owl, hanging by a wing from its owl house.

I saw what happens when girls—who are not supposed to—witness their babies' faces. I saw the helicopters circling like released seeds, their gondola buckets of water dangling. I saw the cattle troughs dry as the Camatta creekbed and cow bodies bulked in the live oak shade. I saw a peregrine falcon tearing the mouse bones, beak to skull, hunger coagulated in its nares. A flatbed truck with whiskey and paper cups, an empty graveyard with a moon big as a belly. Reservoirs turned to sulfur. Pig hooves charred in the barbecue pit. A fifty-three-year-old owl perched in the left ventricle of my heart.

Merlot

new berry old on the vine
sweet enough to pick and touch to your lip
lick the sandust off, see your own reflected mouth
about to swallow it, see your own teeth
large, shovel-tipped, growing larger

grape better before its harvest
sweeter from the harvest knife
stems limp with sun, pregnant
womb of ovular vascular bundles,

how my tongue licks out the septal flesh
each endosperm tasted, each seed
spit into a nearby ditch

| Crossing (ii) |

But maybe she was a boy. I did not look
inside the wrapped rag that spread like a stain
on our trailer ceiling, a pink amoeba shape
that browned and moved closer like hot liquor breath.

For three years,
                I listened to her absence expand
like the magnetic tubes of a solar flare
                                flung outward in a loop
then splattering collapsed on itself.

Suppose one of the pregnant women rose up,
brushed the arroyo willow from the slope of her thighs,
smoothed the live oak twigs in her hand veins,
rose up and told me
        how seven months and showing, she took a sip
        of wine dregs abandoned in the punt of a bottle,
        how the wine became twelve stitches in her lip
        and a ruined womb.

And suppose her words escaped the ringwater like a fawn
born on the wild side of a ravine:

When a whale swallows you, light a fire. Or else descend.

She lay back down and the wind grated her, grains
of her scalp crumbling from her hair, each particle
evanesced to beach bur and brome,
baring toothed leaves and spikelet hands:

—.—

Boy

Skyblue balloons or tags or invitations or granny-knit booties or dumptruck onesies or dinosaur books or plastic-molded China-made tool kits with cute hammers and saws that make saw sounds or cowboy horses or traincars and cabooses and tracks and places to wreck into cars crossing tracks or Barbies that need saving or capturing or innocently de-robing because the Lego men need blankets or some kind of engineering kit that requires putting poles and sticks in holes to make bases for platforms or columns or drumkits assembled and ribboned on Christmas morning or used cars on sixteenth birthdays or socks or candy care packages sent from home to the dorm or the day you rush to a clinic to sit in a waiting room and you don't call your parents while you read a *People* magazine and see the other men or boys waiting as the women or girls look at each other, hear their names called one by one, watch each other walk towards an open door, hoping the next name will not be theirs, or wristwatches you pass on to sons that tick loudly enough in those hours or blue chair-cloth patterns that scratch your arms or the money order you hand the front desk nurse or how you must hold her when she comes out, crying and crying and crying in the car.

What I Leave in Your Palms:

your fingerprints, your hair color change at seven, your shoe size
incrementally rising? I don't think about it, your name
Ash or *Vivi* or *Sarah* or *Chuck*. I don't think
about photographs posted to Facebook, printed, or framed.
I hand them back to you each night for you
to hold. What can I give you to stop threading your face
into my dreams in the guise of new children
in my new marriage? I will give you this: I loved you,
thought of you as I watched the colored-glass mobile
above me. Loved you as a wingless bird.

But I do think of how it might have been
to have let you watch your mother collapse
like a crumpled sheet.
                        I think of leaving you alone with him, a belt
or a *whore* thrown at you, pointed at you like a gun.
I think of nights we might try to leave, fogged up
truck windows while we sleep at a rest stop, rearview mirror angled
at alert so that when it is lit we can start our engine, hope
we have enough gas. My seventeen-year-old self tells you how it is—
how it would be to be seventeen now.

/ Estuary (ii) /

Because the fear began to live
as his steel-toed boots on linoleum,
as the creak in the screen door opening,
as that night the bat got lost between outside
and inside, found a hole between eave and roof edge,
curled itself into a fist, clung to our ceiling tiles

and because the fear became the bat who shook awake
and became its brains broomed onto the wood-paneled walls:

—.—

Chardonnay

Bitch wine. Whore wine. Wine for sluts who wear their hair up
or down too long. Who wear tank tops with jeans over white
thighs. Sweet enough to suck a dick behind your back at a party,
obvious enough on tongue, clings to the throat like your whore
mascara to your lashes. Easy wine for easy girls like you, who want
another glass, another dance with that motherfucker in the vines.
Go on and dance with him then. I'll shotgun this Budweiser
with or without you. Don't give her anymore, would you,
Wade? Jesus. The kind of wine I should tell your mother about,
tell your father how you gulp it from any palm that's offering.
Want more? Here, open your mouth, sweetheart. Let me
pour you a little more, darling. Let me watch it cool your sweat. Let me
put the bottle in your mouth all the way to the neck. Swallow.
Swallow. You know you like it. You know that's why you like it.

Nights

How a bullet. How a blade.

How silver will wink or shine or not.

How we spar the slope sparing the slap.

How a fistful of houseflies breeds,

multiplies like dog shit in an uncleaned yard.

How a rumor skips like a flat stone

over a lake, sinks into your mind,

wedged, undisplaceable slip

of someone's tongue. Netted and tangled.

How a finch. How an avocado rots,

how its skin wrinkles, how the flesh softens,

how the shell holds tight over the pit.

How a glass of vodka grows fuller, how

it disappears. How a throat. How a lampglow

through a window smacks the lawn, soft-lipped

and welcome. How you enter. How you shut

the door behind you. How you let him

slip his hand beneath your shirt, touch

the small of your back, pulling your waist closer.

How the broken dryer buzzes, shakes the laminate

floor. How you return to the sink washing. How

ants trail their own strung sentences. How they end.

How they don't end. How a hollow. How a hole.

/ Halocline (ii) /

That night, before the swell, her father and I watched a meteor
shower from his truck bed in Calf Canyon.

Even as the starshafts smeared over the radiant,
we knew the shine and fade were only debris

burning through the womb of this planet,
that we could never reach out and catch the scraplight from stars,

a wavelength our eyes drink from a place gone black and holed.
The light crawled into the creeksand, snug and paling:

—.—

Animals

dusk-edge he cried *Over here*

    I turned

                    to his voice

       went back to
  collecting these animals   escaped

      who else will

            catch them

roam-eyed bastards, furred

             and furring

    fury of fur

in me   In him

   in between us both

Could she / Could I know

            this forest un-felled
    un-nested of its wasps —   their legs

pumping furiously like a child on a swing,　　　their legs
　　　　six strands of hair waiting
　　　　　　　　　　　　　　　　　　to braid　　　or be
　　braided. Riverblood-hollow
　　　　　　　　　　　muddauber-tunnel-combed
　　　　　　　　so clean
her/my bath run and soaked in until leaked dry
　　　　　　　　This is the story told over
and over while he calls her　　　　　　　from the dusk-edge
　　　　　　　　　　how she hears him
　　　　　　　　　　how she doesn't
　　　　　　　　　　how her womb opens

　　　　　　into her fingers, all blood, all love
　　　all sting,
　　　　　　　　all mudwall
　　　　　　　　　　　　　　house carried
　　　　　　　　　　　　　　in her mouth.

Aubade

Canyon-grass tawny sun rises over its hills pregnant
with all its children, pregnant with asphalt oil and coolant drip,

hot as your anger behind us as we hurtle over Cuesta Grade, two bodies spent,
engine-wrecked, wrench-riddled pocks our scars, white riverbed scab

jagging like a map across our chests. Sunrise glued to our windshield
like insect hearts, insects' veined wings flapping beneath unused wipers.

This morning is the very end, last fragments tucked away inside
manufactured housewalls, dissolved in vodka, burned up in cigarettes

and weed pipes, flamed lighter clicked like a turned-off pistol safety. My name
forever scratched into a wall plank, your name forever scratched into my lung.

Mornings like this, we used to rise and greet the dew-cold grasses with bare feet,
used to throw ourselves into the truck ready to drive vineyard rows, let their mottled

shadows wash over us, let our bodies take each other's space, our legs swinging
into each other, instead of its unkept promise of cold silence, doe-eye black, luster lost

somewhere in its deep taut muscle. Our hearts outpumped, beaten,
bodies like a broom's static on sidewalk. Like a suitcase slung into the trunk

of a rental car. Like a cattle grate rattles its empty song, keeps its cattle.

/ Sound (ii) /

I hear her voice still: tree rings fat with flood and scant with drought,
a rainless creek that deposits the xylem
of her face, the thick muscle of his forearm,
and when I press my thumbnail into the phloem,
it yields like fuzz on sagebrush leaves, like a fontanel:
> reminder of my pinking areolas,
>> still two hands grasping and ungrasping.

Because the frown of her mouth would have been his
chapped lips. Because I would rather scrape out
the redwood bolus than walk toward a receding ocean.

Because the hanged woman in my heart turns:

Pinot Noir

I loved you in your purple womb before I knew you.
Though the task never required it, I would stop in your vineshade
cross-legged among mustard thistle and pick you
berry by berry, slowly at first, then entire clusters, counting
each tooth-stuck multi-seeded embryo until my belly hurt
with fruit-cramp and 105 degrees. You drive me
to the nearest reservoir, tell me to drink the breeze-shake off
the churned waters like a wet dog. You come
out roughly, make me regret your sweet pulp. But o
you slide in so easily, cool soft marble on my thirsty tongue.
How your flesh gives to my teeth, how your skin breaks
every night inside me, one bottle at a time. Saddle up, apply your blinders,
tack in place and jangling, we ride hoof by hoof into the gulf:
how we leave. How we never leave, never leave, never leave.

Crush

I dream we meet: your blue eyes
     a lake I remember we stepped on, frozen,
   its creaking, its stone-fed lighthouse, its light-womb.

     It was Christmas the first time I forgave you:

  we moved your upright piano to the basement
 so you could play, and we could sing together
       in the floorheated concrete. Cocooned in bed
   I knew sadness in you like sadness in an unkempt boxwood.

Maybe/This is how it happened:

    You thought we could get closer, our bodies, not raw enough,
      could get rawer. You thought our limbs
   would be better if they grew thick and emptied
      ready to crash with any wind. And that the not crashing
   would be love.
      Harvest work proved too much—
   you came home with grape-venom

What could I do? I watered the coffee pot
   and fed you what I could.   So, this:

you didn't mean to
   tear out the part of you you didn't like
         by tearing out a part of me
   for the sixth, seventh, eighth, twelfth time you decided:
       love was my heart,
              the size of your fist.

Each time like a song
   we used to write down to this wick   I knew was burning inside you.

  How we used to let it burn like a crow
    folded up into a stitch in snow.
             or let it burn like ——.

    let it burn white like stars when we sat in the hot springs, not knowing

it was −5 degrees out, not knowing all the tree limbs
      were encased in ice. Until we heard, at 2 a.m.,

the iced boughs crash
     and wondered at our bodies,
              still full of blood, still warm with meat.

Author's Acknowledgments

Thanks to the Kentucky Foundation for Women, who provided support toward the creation of this book. Thanks to all those who speak up and speak out.

Much gratitude to Brain Mill Press for their thoughtfulness and care with these poems. Thanks, too, to Kiki Petrosino for her words.

And, always, thanks and love to my *stella polaris*, Bryan.

About the Author

Kentucky poet, folklorist, and educator Sarah McCartt-Jackson has been published by *Indiana Review*, *Journal of American Folklore*, *The Maine Review*, *Tidal Basin Review*, *NANO Fiction*, *Bellingham Review*, and others. She is the recipient of an Al Smith Individual Artist Fellowship from the Kentucky Arts Council and has served as artist-in-residence for the Great Smoky Mountains National Park and Shotpouch Cabin through Oregon State University. She is the author of *Stonelight*, which won the 2017 Airlie Prize, and two chapbooks, *Vein of Stone* and *Children Born on the Wrong Side of the River*, which won the 2015 Mary Ballard Poetry Prize. She works on a farm in Louisville.

www.ingramcontent.com/pod-product-compliance
Lightning Source LLC
Chambersburg PA
CBHW051334110526
44591CB00026B/2996